Matter

by Kim Fields

Matter

All things are made of matter. Matter has mass and takes up space. Think about your bedroom. Your bed, clothes, and toys are made of matter.

Even things you cannot see are
made of matter. Air is a kind of matter.

All things made of matter have mass.
Mass is how much matter is in an object.
Matter is made of tiny parts. You can see
the tiny parts of matter through a microscope.

Properties of Matter

Matter has different properties. You can observe a **property** using your senses. Some properties are color, size, shape, and weight.

One property of matter is weight.
Which of these is light?
Which of these is heavy?

You can see and touch some properties of matter.

Matter can feel smooth or rough. This seashell feels smooth. Sandpaper feels rough.

The seashell has a spiral shape. The sandpaper is shaped like a square.

Another property of matter is size.
This beach ball is big. The golf ball is small.
Color is a property of matter. What colors
can you see on this beach ball?

States of Matter

The three **states of matter** are solid, liquid, and gas.

Solids

A **solid** has its own shape and size. A solid also has mass and takes up space.

A table is a solid. Your pencils and erasers are also solids. They all have a size, shape, and weight.

You can measure the size of some solids with a ruler.

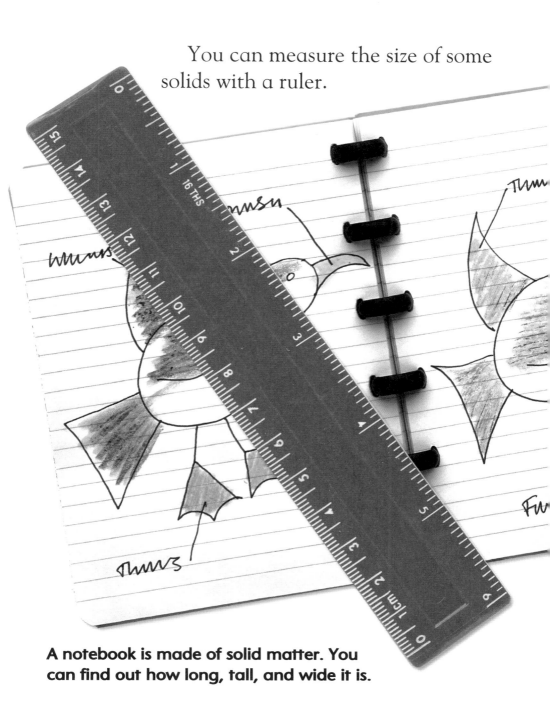

A notebook is made of solid matter. You can find out how long, tall, and wide it is.

Liquids

A **liquid** is a kind of matter without a shape. A liquid takes the shape of the container that holds it. Liquids have mass and take up space.

Milk is a liquid. It takes the shape of the carton or jug that holds it. Pour milk into a glass. Now it takes the shape of the glass.

A liquid can be measured using a measuring cup. You can pour milk into a measuring cup to find its volume. The amount of space a liquid takes up is called its volume.

A measuring cup measures the amount of space taken up by a liquid.

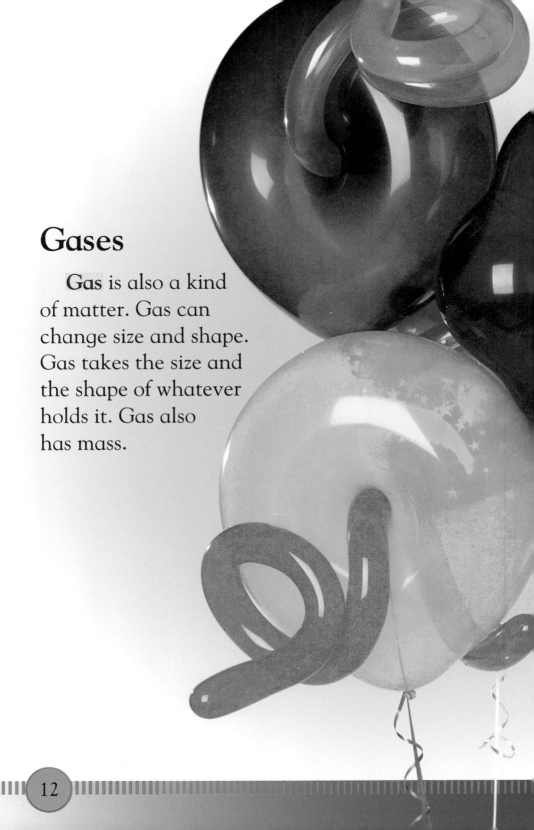

Gases

Gas is also a kind of matter. Gas can change size and shape. Gas takes the size and the shape of whatever holds it. Gas also has mass.

The air you blow into
a balloon is made of gases.
You cannot see the gases.
They take up space, but they
have no shape of their own.

Changing Matter

There are many ways to change matter.
Matter can change in size.
It can get bigger or smaller.

The size of matter can change. Take some bites out of an apple. Now the apple is a different size!

Matter can change in shape.
It can become round or square.
It can become flat or bumpy.

You can change dough into many shapes.

Mixing and Separating Matter

A **mixture** is something made of two or more things. The things you put in a mixture do not change.

These marbles are a mixture of colors. The marbles are also a mixture of sizes.

You can separate a mixture
into its parts. Each marble
can be taken out one at a time.
You can separate the yellow marbles
from the green marbles.

Mixing with Water

Water is used to make some mixtures. You can separate these mixtures in different ways. Put oil and water together. The water sinks and the oil floats.

Mix sugar and water. If you heat this mixture, the water can separate by evaporating.

Oil floats on water.

Sugar mixes with water.

Cooling Matter

Fruit juice is liquid matter. It can change when you cool it. Pour juice into molds. Put the molds into the freezer. The juice in each mold will turn into a frozen treat. Then it will be a solid.

Air contains water vapor. Water vapor is a gas. Water vapor can change from a gas to a liquid. When water vapor touches something cold, it changes to liquid drops of water.

Water vapor from a kettle touches cold glass and changes into drops of water.

Water can also change from a liquid to a solid. This liquid rain changed to solid ice when it got very cold.

Rainwater drips from the roof and freezes. It changes into solid ice.

Heating Matter

Heating can change a solid into a liquid. Chocolate is a solid. When chocolate is heated, it melts. Melted chocolate is a liquid.

Heating can change a liquid into a gas.

When you light a candle, the candle wax gets hot. It melts and turns into liquid wax.

The liquid wax gets hotter and turns into a gas. This is why the candle gets smaller!

Glossary

gas   matter that has mass and takes the shape and size of its container

liquid   matter that takes up space, has mass, and takes the shape of its container

mass   the amount of matter in an object

mixture   two or more things with different properties that can be separated

property   something about matter that you can observe with your senses

solid   matter that has mass and its own size and shape

states of matter the different forms matter can take: solid, liquid, or gas